abandon

RECkless

www.fourward.ca

1

Known for the artistic edge and spirited approach she brings to leadership, development, and collaborative projects, Karen Driedger has worked across Canada in the field of recreation, leisure and wellness. Providing services for educational initiatives, recreational organizations, community development and entrepreneurial ventures, she's a master at the art of creative solutions, building meaningful connections through learning, living, leadership and leisure. Karen entices exploration and action through *fourward*, a collaborative experience.

Library and Archives Canada Cataloguing in Publication
Driedger, Karen, 1963-
  Reckless abandon / Karen Driedger.
ISBN 978-0-9865390-0-8
  1. Creative ability. 2. Play. I. Title.
BF408.D75 2010   153.3'5   C2010-901325-5

A portion of all proceeds donated to the Florence Centre, Zaporizhia, Ukraine A Family Service & Community Education Centre, one of the 1st non-governmental public organizations in Zaporizhya. http://florence-eng.ucoz.ua/. Philosophy: to serve community, groups and individuals to improve quality of life. See the last page to see how they creatively connect people with play.

Satisfy your Snack Attack with our Snack Series ~ Creative Connections

RECkless Abandon – Connecting PEOPLE with PLAY

Nourishing Facts
Valeur nutritive

Amount/Teneur

	%DV/%VQ
Fun/Amuser Over 150 pages of good fun	100%
Saturated/satures with tidbits to nourish your creativity	100%

Information Per 1 card

Connecting People with Play	from start to finish
Connecting work with play	somewhere in the middle
Linking home and play	somewhere near the end

Creative Connections Per 1 card

	Unlimited
Ideas	U count
Connections	U connect

Creative Calories ∞

% Daily Value/% valeur quotidienne: Vit Sparks 33% Vit Smiles 33% Question Marks 33% Zoning out .9%

Ingredients: Ideas, pictures, words, colours, creative connections.

Good health comes from PLAYING. JOUER contribuent a une bonne sante.

www.fourward.ca

3

You've gotta get to know Dave!
He's a suit with a personality.
He infuses laughter, cuts to the chase, creates controversy, builds solutions.
He's a closer. He also gives the author the space and support to explore, expand & travel.

Who?

Dedicated to Dave

A **Special Thanks** to all of **U** who I've collaborated with along the way.

Thanks to all who have thought

here we go once again.
dreamer, dreamer,
Monday morning schemer.
Another one, two, three,
how many will it take for her to see
that this won't go anywhere
How Dare
she think
these ideas
are more than just fun and folly
like Bolly
Wood
Could
that all who have rolled their eyes, laughed and joked,
know
that thanks be to them
for their persuasion when
just before the idea is dropped
and all is but stopped
the laughs and the jokes
stroke one, two, three
chords to carry on
piss off who I can
continue to dream and bomb and carry on.

how exciting this new energy.
ideas, ideas,
ideas galore.
They soar
rich with passion and fervor
where will they go
oh
look how she moves
foUrward
learning
living
leading a charge
leisurely and large
with less on the outside
Below the surface
the purpose
clearing, calming, coming
going, being
In the moment
smiling and knowing
something but nothing
the search is still going
On to the sea
where new we will see

Thanks to all who have thought

www.fourward.ca

WALK IT Pepper

Remember the sound the teacher on Charlie Brown made? Standing in a lecture hall myself I sometimes I hear Charlie's teacher, ARRRRGH!

Then I reminded myself to walk the talk. I was stuck. I didn't quite know how this 'book' was going to turn out, or what it was for. It turned into a buzzcard, a sample of my work. And it's the first of a creative connections series.

It transformed through discussion, collaboration, risk-taking and creative thinking. This thing that started as a book is now a sample of my work. Through using the process that I use with others, one that's collaborative, that twists thinking and pushes boundaries, we transformed an idea into creative action. Eureka! wehadababyitsaboy

Thanks Guy(s) & Gals for prodding, poking, talking and joking.

RECkless Abandon

Throw off your shoes, run across the grass, lie down and stare at the sky...

at work or home, with others or alone.

Not sure this is going to be for me. I'm not much for bare feet.

Loosen up, take them off, keep them on, no matter. Are you willing to open up to new ideas?

Okay so listen to this one, they call me up, it's Saturday night and they need a goalie. I didn't really want to but it was the guys. I felt guilty and so I said yes. I mean I love getting out but Saturday night, come on, I had plans an...

Whooooa, don't need the whole story! It's those strings attached that are a pain...Goalie huh?

When did you play last?

Not because...

☆ they needed a goalie, your kids wanted to

☆ you were stressed out

☆ the doctor told...

U2

Just for the fun of it?

Do YOU like to PLAY?

Play: To occupy oneself in amusement, sport, or other recreation
(www.thefreedictionary.com)

Play: to be of free mind, free body, free spirit   Play: to jump from one rock to another

Play: to move into another world   Play: to imagine   Play: to be childlike

Play: to feel no pressure   Play: to toy with ideas, actions, movements, interactions

Play: to dream   Play: to pursue   Play: to travel

Play: to do whatever you want to do

Play: to explore new ideas and creations   Play: to pretend   Play: to act Play: to

piss adults off Play: to run through a field of flowers Play: to build a garage

Play: to completely lose any inhibitions Play: to splash   Play: to laugh until you cry

Play: (what does it mean to you?) _____

11

Physically play so that your body remembers the feeling of freedom.

Dance

canoe Skip hockey Tag shed Underwater Lacrosse Cricket Sport Volleyball darts Build Hike Games Fooseball ball rope Tango kite Ski

goose Paint Dodgehouse Patty soccer yoga fly play fit Construct Revolution Recreation Duck Billiards Jive duck Swim sculpt cake

When was the last time your mind played?

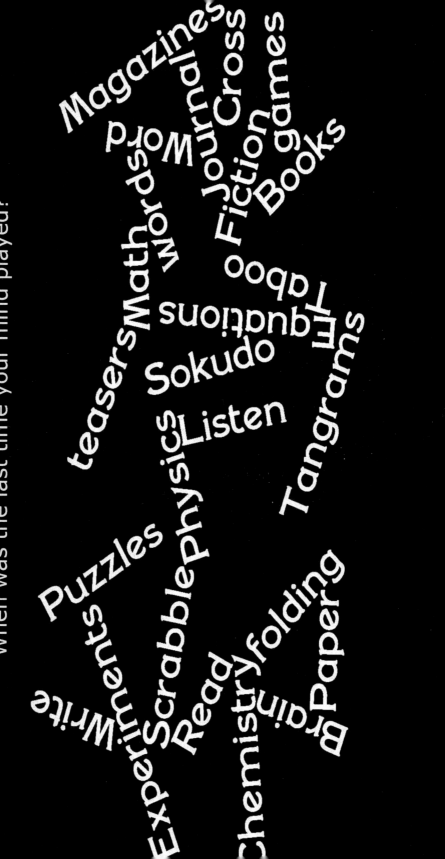

Emotional and spiritual play happens when watching Cirque de Soleil, attending religious ceremony, meditating or when walking through the woods.

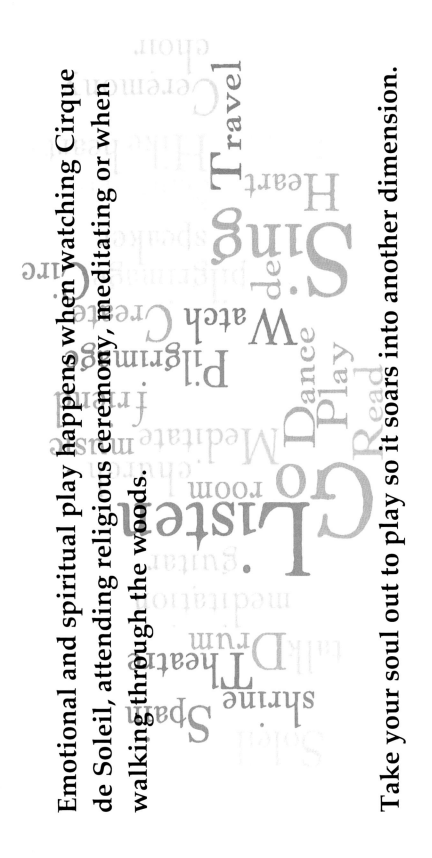

Take your soul out to play so it soars into another dimension.

Free play, unstructured, imaginative play:

Play with no rules, playing make believe or role playing social situations.
It is crucial for normal development.

play

Build

Dress

Leggo

Act

Play

blocks

Role

up

Dance

boxes

Make your own Wordle www.wordle.net

Value PLAY highly - it is fundamental to our success!

PLAY makes us more **socially adept.**   helps us **work through** anxiety and *stress.* **builds** our **cognitive** skills, things like **problem solving.** play **promotes** *neural* **development** in "higher" **brain** areas involved in emotional reactions and social **learning.** scientists reported in 2003 that **play fighting** releases brain-derived neurotrophic factor (BDNF)—a protein that **stimulates** the growth of new neurons—in these regions. play makes us **better adjusted, smarter** and less stressed. "a child who has had a rich exposure to social play experiences is more likely to become an adult who can manage **unpredictable** social *situations.*" it has a prominent role in biology, **education** and **life.** play-deprivation is **serious** stuff, it can keep children from growing into **happy,** well-adjusted adults. and can help not so well-adjusted adults (who's well adjusted these days?) **develop** into more **well-adjusted** human beings. *1 hour* of meaningful play and imagination (community drama, acting out roles in society) = growth in **negotiation,** social roles and **co he si on.** play is **purposeful,** it can be **practical,** even if the purpose and practicality is **purely** fun! Some Refs: Scientific American Mind, February2009, Serendip/SciSoc, 2005, "Nurture Shock"

How many books
have you read
in the past month?

| 0 | 0.1 | .25 | 1 | 2 | 3 |

Rate your favourite
book on a
Scale of 0 to 3

Why play?

To relax
To escape
To learn
To socialize
To compete
To _____

What
does
play IDEALLY look
like to
you?

Attitude vs Attitude

Play-Inclined	Play-Averse
Spontaneous	Structured
Rule breaker	Rule keeper
Explorer	Home-body
Curious	Content
Open to new ideas	Closed-minded
Find humour in situations	Find frustration
Life is lighthearted	Life is serious
Laugh	Cry
Trusting	Skeptical

What if you are both?
Most of us are.

What if you are MORE Play-Averse?
Choose to be MORE Play-Inclined.

"The unexamined life is not worth living." Socrates
Are you willing to play?

Examine, choose carefully & get on with it!

Don't

give up play as a luxury when things get serious

!

It is never too late to start: play promotes continued mental and physical well-being of adults. It is well documented, scientifically proven, and innately our nature. **Take it seriously.**

Dolphin or Dinosaur. Which are you, adaptable, extinct or maybe **DISTINCT**?
If you stay in the same patterns it won't take long for you to go the way of Tyrannosaurus Rex. **What would that be like?** Creepy?

Create a space in your head, notice your thoughts to bolster your ability to play.

playful exploration

1. Make it a **game** – everything, from brushing your teeth to working on a project at school or work

2. An hour with **no rules** – check your assumptions about rules written and unwritten. If you are at home in the evening the lights are on, that's the rule. So turn them off, sit in the dark, use a flashlight or candles. OR instead of sitting at your desk, stand at it all day.

3. **No time** like no time – spend a day without a watch, black berry or cell phone. Pressures of how to use time, being productive, appointments, being on time are hammered into us.

4. Watch **kids**, play with them, act like one. Crawl, sit on the floor, play on monkey bars and with blocks. Research shows that kids who play with blocks develop better language skills.

5. Find **humour** for five minutes. Next time you're in a meeting choose 5 minutes to conduct a study. Find the humour in everything for that 5 minutes. 6. Take a **day off** – of being an adult.

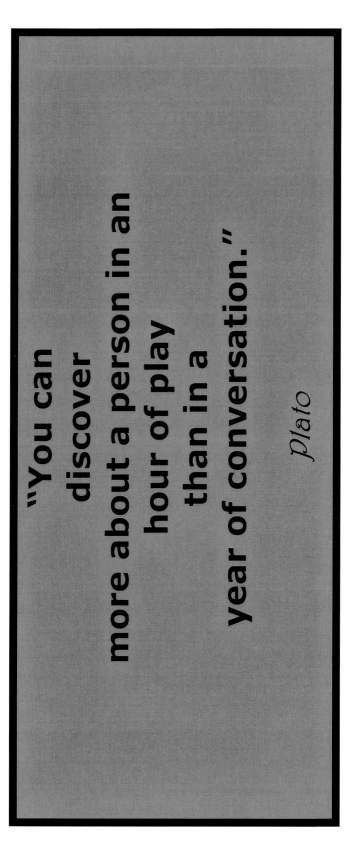

"You can discover more about a person in an hour of play than in a year of conversation."

Plato

www.fourward.ca

Capture IT

What gets measured gets done. Use ways to see the impact, results, changes & challenges.

2 ways

ONE – not your usual Journal

Take a journal to work; The one with the journal is the observer, looking at play from the outside. Pass it around the office, record memorable moments with words, pictures, or items like a scrapbook. Jot key words during meetings and create powerful poems. Read them to the group at the end of the session. Use it to build a prototype, newsletter or an idea bank.

Start one with a friend to record adventures, or catch phrases. It's a great way to connect. **WRight Now** write down your thoughts and ideas, one sentence, one word, a picture, a punctuation mark...your ideas, ideas of how to increase and use play. Plan how to use it. If it doesn't work stop, drop and roll, burn it, build it differently or try something else.

Become in a **handwriting analyst**, people LOVE to hear about themselves, a great party trick!

TWO – be a photographer

Bring a camera with you everywhere. Email pictures out. Make a storyboard. Make one of a great day, adventures. Buy a couple of disposable cameras to share around. Get others to take pictures throughout the day/session, pass them around so everyone takes pictures...

Have theme photo shots; anything on the **edge** or **hair** or **prototypes** or **bright colours**...
PLAY WITH the IDEA, bring it to WORK, SCHOOL, CHURCH?

Warm-up to IT

Play around

Follow the leader – at home, in an elevator, at the office or when shopping. Be the follower and the leader. It's amazing how people mirror others in order to communicate better. Mirror someone and then try to get them to mirror your stance, position, hand gestures. Make it your **spysperiment**.

Clapping - How often do you start clapping because others are? A standing ovation begins with one or two or twenty people standing up and the crowd follows. Start clapping and see who joins you, during an exercise class, in a movie, at work, with your kids. Who doesn't like a little Synapse Blast every once in awhile?

When you clap the synapses in your brain fire engaging and stimulating both the left and right hemispheres of the brain which wakes up your whole being.

23

www.fourward.ca

Recreation Therapy

Janet Griffin is a Recreation Therapist in Ontario, Canada. She uses **Patty Cake** as a mindfulness experiential exercise "with the goal of developing and/or increasing self-awareness for patients who have experienced trauma. I use the exercise to talk about the dynamics that are created in the context of social relationships, create awareness of habitual patterns...and personal responses to change. Through mindful attention to their own response throughout the exercise, patients [can] experience habitual responses, gain perspective through discussing the historical roots of different behaviour patterns and defenses, have an open conversation about the impact of their behaviour on others, have the opportunity to try newer ways of relating to others and learn to tolerate their affective response to healthier ways of relating." For some it creates laughter and positive memories, for others it "triggers intense feelings of fear and anxiety as the experience of games triggers memories of past abuse that happened in the context of "play". As patients couple their engagement in the exercise with safety and grounding skills, they have the opportunity for a corrective experience wherein the act of playing as an adult gets associated with safety, support and empowerment."

Powerful!

How do you get to work?

Skip (school), Run, Dance, Saunter like a model, ipod Shuffle, Scooter (Susan Sarandon does), Bus or Train (stare at others), Bike (like a bat outta hell), Drive (playing the music or a book or playing with ideas in your head)...

It Matters because it's the reference for your day, like breakfast or no breakfast, nourishment or no nourishment, play, no play, Creative energy, no Creative energy.

Pic is from Google office, too cool!

Don't have enough?

Abandoned recreation

Pic Hotel California, Todos Santos, Mexico. "You can check in anytime you want but you can never leave."

What the h... is this Hotel California thing about?

People get caught up in a lifestyle and can't change.

www.fourward.ca

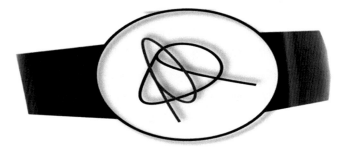

Look at the
TIME!

www.fourward.ca

The inner workings

People with shrinking time for recreation are less satisfied and less happy with life.

In 2006, 33% of respondents in Alberta, Canada said they didn't have enough time to participate in local recreation.
(Romsa Journal of Leisure Research, ARPA 2006)

What are all those Cowboys & Cowgirls doing?

Other reasons Canadians give for Abandoning Recreation:

- lack of awareness/info
- price
- facilities (no supply)

Time is one of the top.

Timekeepers have evolved. Watches – are going out of style, who wears a watch when you've got

Cell phones!!! Blackberries, IPhones, Laptops, IPods

Clocks, sure we still have those and

Bell Towers still chime in mature neighbourhoods, the ones we want to live in but they're so expensive! Older churches beckon our attendance with wonderful chimes Sunday morning.

School Bells buzz keeping children ON TIME for recess, lunch, and other important appointments, like the bus ride home.

Sun Dials are erected as landmarks and plopped in gardens as ornaments,

Hourglasses are making a comeback, $38.00 @ your local Chapters.

www.fourward.ca

The notion and perception of time has evolved. "The 5 minute manager", "The 4 hour work week", "5 Where will you be five years from today?" time management, daylight savings time, fast food, the slow movement, twittering, video on demand. We're convenient, we're trying to conserve energy, our own. We've done well.

Obesity rates sky high, juvenile diabetes increasing at an alarming rate. Dr. Jennifer James says that 'time is the new currency.' Great we've all got the same amount.

The only currency I know is the mighty $, donaro, peso, hard cold cash! Cha ching!

Is Time the new currency or is it Attitude? Or Creativity?

Interesting...so we're all equal, bank accounts on par, no one will EVER have MORE or LESS than the person next to them.

Interesting...pack in as much as possible, multi-task. The

generation that grew up with Sesame Street (Gen Xers, those born between 1962-1975) started this journey to evolving the multi-tasked brain.

Lots of cool stuff about generational stuff: http://www.urbandictionary.com/define.php?term=Sesame%20Street%20generation

Then came the Net gen with computers at home, at school. They are hardwired for multi-tasking. Net Genners can be texting, driving, changing the channel on the radio, talking with a buddy sitting next to them, putting on their mascara, smoking a cigarette – wait, no they don't smoke, okay drinking a Coke Zero, and be thinking about where their next world tour will take them – all at once without the blink of an eye.

Whereas the Boomers, anyone over 40, find it difficult to chew gum and walk.

www.fourward.ca

Interesting...Snack Culture, small blurbs in short bursts, with catchy colours and lots of variety, many screens, options, pictures, ideas, complex not in carbohydrates (information) because information is easy to access. It's the white bread, the pasta, the potatoes and rice and all those things that we used to pile on our plates. But now, it is not about information anymore. NO CARBS! We've got low carb wraps, white bread has been taking a hit in the marketplace, potatoes and rice THEY are responsible for our gluttonous behaviour that's gotten us into this obese state. TOO MUCH INFORMATION!

NOW it's about the complexity of the organic salad, combining vegetables and fruit in a delicate blend so as to bring out the natural flavours. High in vitamins, anti-oxidants, minerals and many medicinal qualities, we delight in a salad for lunch. We snack on organic carrots bought from the Hutterites at the Farmer's Market, if we take the time to venture out or we grow our own on the small plot we've decided to plow or get them from the community garden where residents gather to plant and grow food because it's healthy, the price is right and it's fresh.

Information is all around us, it's a dime a dozen so now it's about the exotic, the deeper essence, we're moving up the monkey ladder to a higher existence.

The Net Generation won't compromise their Leisure time. Lazy I don't think so, SMART you bet! They not only value it, they LIVE IT (play). Cirque du Soleil: The Spark ~ Igniting the Creative Fire that Lives within Us All a book by John U. Bacon, a journalist, is a fable that tells of Bacon's sojourn with Cirque. In it Cirque-ers say that creativity and safety are of utmost importance, they will not compromise either therefore they have 100% creativity and 100% safety.

www.fourward.ca

VOILA – now we are focused on deciphering and connecting, creating a whole new world. Different than the past 40 or 50 years, but not so different. My grandmother made her own soap, not because it would be cool to give away ginger asparagus soap at Christmas but because she had to. Cloth bags to the grocer or market were the only way to carry the fresh produce home, saving the planet was second to nourishing the family.

Did you know that a 'jiffy' is an actual unit of time for 1/100th of a second!

Interesting...we all have 24 hours in a day.

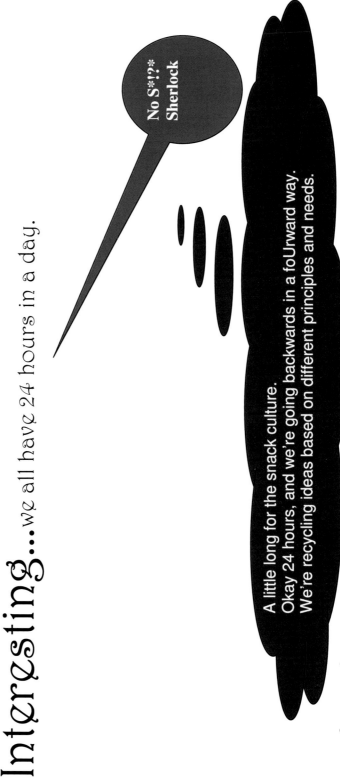

No S*!?* Sherlock

A little long for the snack culture.
Okay 24 hours, and we're going backwards in a foUrward way.
We're recycling ideas based on different principles and needs.

www.fourward.ca

The disappearance of time
This wonderful guy with a killer last name

Mihaly Csikszentmihalyi is a Hungarian psychology professor who has devoted his life's work to the study of what makes people truly happy, satisfied and fulfilled. He's the architect of the

FLOW theory

It's when the level of challenge meets with the skill level creating a perfect match and one is able to be 'in the zone.'

The existential elements of play.

Ya okay but what does this have to do with play?

"being completely involved in an activity for its own sake. The ego falls away. Time flies. Every action, movement, and thought follows inevitably from the previous one, like playing jazz. Your whole being is involved, and you're using your skills to the utmost."

Time stands still, you don't give a rat's behind about anything, just doing what it is that you are doing...AHHHHHH to be in the flow zone

If only we could

www.fourward.ca

stop time

we can take out the batteries, shut off the phone

suspend time

lay the hourglass on its side

get into *FLOW* mode

Wait what about all our great inventions??????

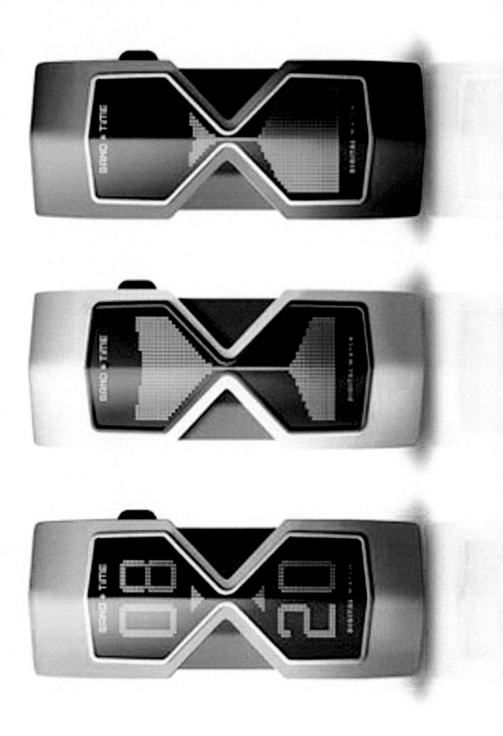

"Everywhere is within walking distance if you have the time."
Steven Wright

Remember walking to school? If you're under 30 you won't.

Remember riding bike in the back lane without a helmet? If you're under 20 you won't.

Remember going to visit your neighbour down the block? If you're under 20 you likely won't because most North Americans don't know their neighbours.

Remember playing street hockey and yelling 'car', grabbing the nets, hauling them to the side of the road, letting the car pass then resuming a game on a cold winter evening, when it's dark and there are no street lights? If you're under 30 you likely won't because 'the world has changed'.

Remember your parents telling you to go outside and play, without them, in the evening, and not to come in until it's bed time? Likely not if you are in the Net Generation.

Are we **safe?**

Yes & No

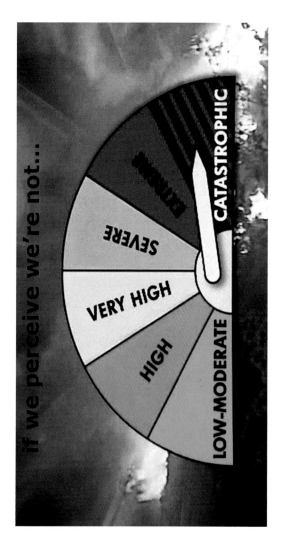

if we perceive we're not...

www.fourward.ca

Times have changed and we're working on how to make our streets safer for everyone.

Better lighting, front porches, Citizens on Patrol, cul de sacs, Bloc Parents. **What about slower vehicles and narrower streets? How about more street parties and getting to know your neighbours?** The Walking School Bus concept is a great example. People gather together, one parent is the 'driver' who walks the kids to school.

By twisting our thinking, turning ideas sideways and harvesting creative solutions we can build stronger communities, ones that we can play in safely.

So what about all our great inventions??? **Keep inventing!!!**

> Humanity has advanced, when it has advanced, not because it has been sober, responsible, and cautious, but because it has been playful, rebellious, and immature. Tom Robbins

TWISTED THINKING ~ a BARREL OF MONKEYS & JUICY FRUIT

"The creation of something new is not accomplished by the intellect but by the play instinct acting from inner necessity. The creative mind plays with the objects it loves." Carl Jung

What would you expect to find in a yellow barrel of monkeys game container?
Plastic monkeys
What if you found smooth stones?

What would you expect to find in a juicy fruit container?
Juicy Fruit gum, mmmm that fresh smell of juicy fru...
What if you found chocolate chips? maybe better

What if you found the unexpected? What if you looked for the unexpected?
It's like seeing someone who is wearing a suit and tie walking down the road carrying a briefcase; you'd think he was going to work or a business meeting. Maybe he's an actor. Or if a woman was wearing a short, tight mini-skirt with high spike heels on the street corner at midnight you may assume that she's a prostitute. Maybe SHE's an actor. **LOOK 4 the Unexpected.** We put **2** and **2** together based on our experiences, societal values, what we read, who we talk with.
www.fourward.ca

47

Quality of Life

Rate your quality of life between 1 – 9

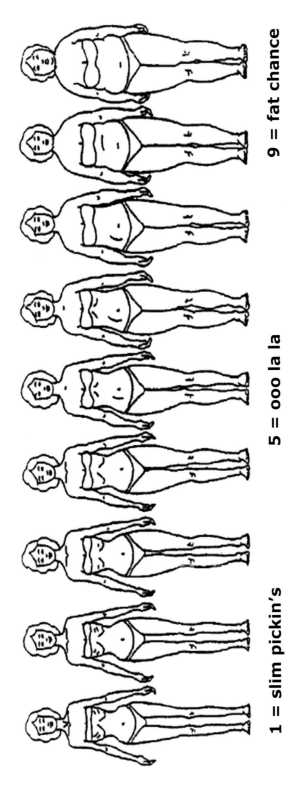

1 = slim pickin's

5 = ooo la la

9 = fat chance

THREE CHOICES

1. Is leisure more important than work?

2. Is work more important than leisure?

3. Are they equal?

For me it's leisure. Why do you work? Is it so you can afford to play?

No Brainer! Work, work, work. Need money man.

Importance of Leisure and Work
Alberta, Canada
2006, Harper

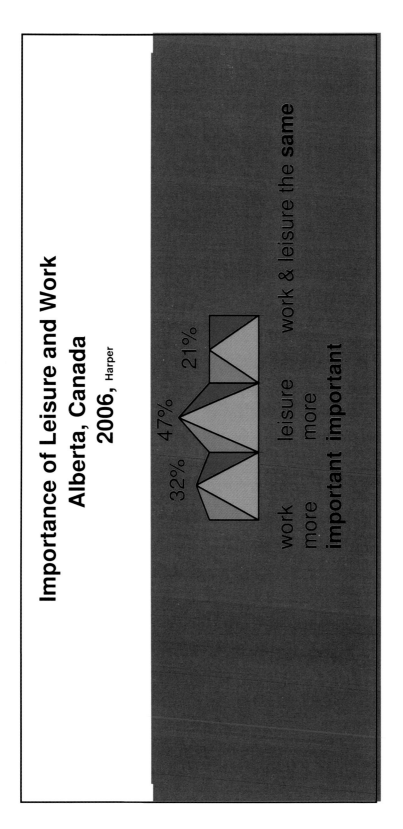

32%   47%   21%

work more **important**   leisure more important   work & leisure the **same**

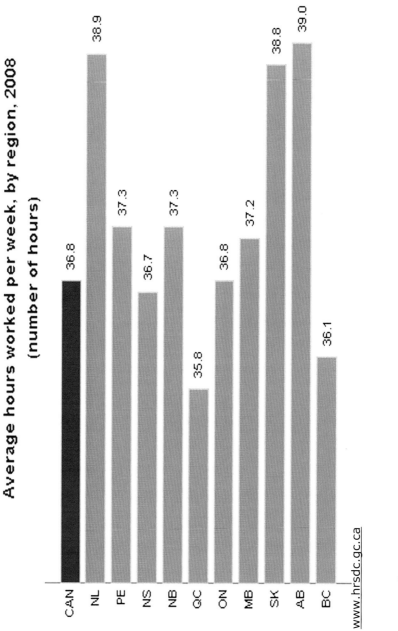

Average hours worked per week, by region, 2008 (number of hours)

Region	Hours
CAN	36.8
NL	38.9
PE	37.3
NS	36.7
NB	37.3
QC	35.8
ON	36.8
MB	37.2
SK	38.8
AB	39.0
BC	36.1

www.**fou**rward.ca

Riiiiight...

What's up with these guys?

Must've been called in from the guild. I guess she needed a different 'Look', what can we learn from these guys?

BIG Variation between Canadian provinces.

Check out **Newfoundlanders** they're hard at work and play.

We know that "People who value leisure above work are happier, healthier and more satisfied with life than those who rate work first." Harper, 2006

How about Alberta? Albertans who put leisure before work has risen 20% since 1996. Yahoo! But wait, they're working the most and have the least leisure time...this doesn't make sense.

Across Canada over the past 8 years leisure time has been decreasing and work time has been increasing. People are saying it's important but doing the opposite.

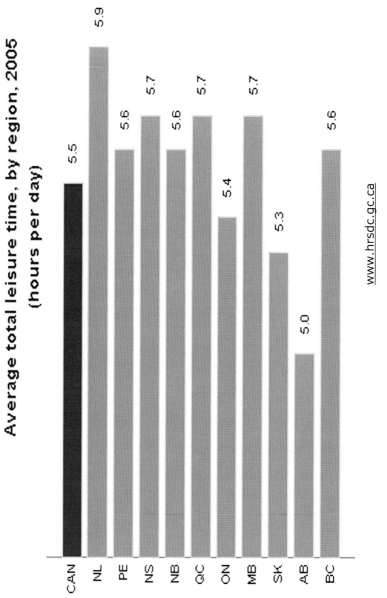

Average total leisure time, by region, 2005
(hours per day)

Region	Hours
CAN	5.5
NL	5.9
PE	5.6
NS	5.7
NB	5.6
QC	5.7
ON	5.4
MB	5.7
SK	5.3
AB	5.0
BC	5.6

www.hrsdc.gc.ca

www.fourward.ca

Leisure satisfaction

contributes to overall

...Life satisfaction...

Getting SATISFACTION

I can't get no...

So check your attitude.

Age is the only demographic variable that is a significant predictor of leisure satisfaction – the younger you are the better it is. Can't change your age.

Health – the healthier you are the better it is, so you know the drill

Volume of participation in leisure activities – the more you take part the better you'll feel.

Leisure activity repertoire (number of different activities participated in) – expand your repertoire! Try something new.

Leisure attitude – the "I can't, won't, don't want to" will stomp all over your SATISFACTION. This one makes all the difference in the world, you can change it.

Romsa, Journal of Leisure Research

55

Check it

Checklists, now you're talkin'

List people you'll like this!

Make a Checklist of what's important to you.

Do something meaningful, physically active, committed to something, keep busy, do lots of different things, relax and take it easy, something different from work/school, be spontaneous, compete with self or others, laugh and enjoy, make use of my skills, improve skills, develop skills, have something to show for my efforts, get approval for what I do, be successful, have a feeling of personal worth, learn more about myself, develop interpersonal relationships, be part of a group/team, meet new people, develop friendships, help others, be in attractive surroundings.

Even though leisure is treasured there is a trend towards less time for recreation and play. Shrinking discretionary time leaves us less play time therefore lower life satisfaction and happiness.

Play to improve quality of life and wellbeing.

Indicators of Well-being in Canada, HRDC Canada

Well-being

Family Life

Social Participation

Housing

Leisure

Work

Health

Learning

Security

Financial Security

Environment

Human Resources and Skills Development Canada put together10 **Indicators of Well-being in Canada. Leisure** is related to all of them. **Health** – many leisure activities contribute to health, physical (sports, walking) and mental (stress reduction). **Security** – the stronger you are mentally and physically the more able you are to take care of yourself. When people recreate in the neighbourhood together there is safety in numbers and friendships gained through leisure activities provides support. **Environment** – many leisure activities are based in natural environments therefore provide support to preserving and conservation efforts. Trails and parks are two. **Financial security** – your overall wellbeing is influenced by health, willingness to learn and social participation, if you are healthy and happy you will be better able to work and be financially secure. **Learning** – we learn through play, through games, art and socializing we learn leadership and social skills, problem-solving and decision-making, communication, hand-eye coordination and gross motor skills. **Work** – the more satisfied we are with our leisure time the more satisfied we are overall so when we head out to work we're happier to be there and more productive. **Housing** – Where you live and the quality of housing influence wellbeing, how does leisure relate? Your location dictates in part, the types of activities accessible to you, if you're close to a lake kayaking is out your door, if downtown potential for purple recreation (i.e. drugs) increases. **Family life** – playing together as a family unit, hiking, skiing, can give families quality time together. **Social participation** – many leisure activities take place in centres with others. Craft shows, soccer games, music concerts and going out for supper all involve social interaction.

www.fourward.ca

RULES

Games have rules set up in advance and followed. Some believe that play doesn't have a priori of rules, so more creative responses can happen. However, play has rules too usually unwritten. Take playing house, there are certain roles & boundaries that are culturally determined. Trust is needed in order to play & be creative. Improv theatre seems spontaneous but there are rules that govern it too (see page 104 for Ten Commandments of Improv).

Rules R good, WHAT? These aren't rules!

RULES for play:
1. Go with it – don't over think it, we learn from it, it's instinctual.
2. Be kind – with others and yourself.
Make up your own after that!

I like making up rules & breaking them

Charlie Steffens, Spencer Gorin conducted a 'Healthy Play' research study in 2005. They discuss how play and rules can reduce aggression & acting out, increase nurturing, social skills, communication, peer mediation, conflict resolution...

Their Philosophy: Why do we play? To **Have Fun**
The most important part of every game? **People**
At the end of each game they have a quiet reflection time to share only positive comments about others and the game.

Their 2 Rules of Play:
1. If anyone is hurt either physically or emotionally, the closest person must stop playing and take care of that person.
2. If 2 people have a disagreement, the two people involved need to leave the game until they come up with a peaceful solution.

www.fourward.ca

Yes there is a Theory of Play

http://serendip.brynmawr.edu/playground/theory.html

Which contends that:

- **there's NOT a lot of difference between playing and learning**
- **exploring** is the underpinning
- **enjoyment** is inherent
- **play develops motor, cognitive and social skills**

The American Academy of Pediatrics Reports:

Play allows children to use their creativity while developing their imagination, dexterity, and physical, cognitive, and emotional strength. Play is important to healthy brain development. It is through play that children at a very early age engage and interact in the world around them. Play allows children to create and explore a world they can master, conquering their fears while practicing adult roles, sometimes in conjunction with other children or adult caregivers.

WARNING:

Play is not hazardous to your health. Continue to play while pregnant or breast-feeding. While you may experience enjoyable side effects such as laughing, smiling, peace and happiness, continue to play. Recommended at work, home and school, in public, private, inside, outside, for old and young.

Health fun and games are available through:
- **local internet connections**
- **retail stores worldwide**

Recommended sites:

- www.gamesforhealth.org – information on Exer-gaming. Visit their *Hopelab* – where 'Re-mission' a video game for teens with cancer has shown results of higher levels of knowledge and better adherence to treatment regimes.

- www.healthgamesresearch.org – for research on video games.

Games like Wii Fit include aerobics, balance, hula hoop, bowling and more.

Great for seniors, injury rehabilitation, intergenerational cohesion, parties and conferences (great for breaks!).

63

www.fourward.ca

"Forget not that the earth delights to feel your bare feet and the winds long to play with your hair."

Kahlil Gibran

How To's and What To Do's

TAKE A DEEP BREATH
Take your shoes off, plant yourself firmly on the ground.

Close your eyes and visualize the feeling of:
- cool grass under your feet
- hot sand burning your instep
- warm mud squishing between your toes

Remember the sensation of simple steps.

65

SMILES Everyone

Smiling

Practice

In 1960 class pictures at a girls' school were analysed for genuine smiles. Decades later the ones with genuine smiles had happier lives, better health, and were in stable relationships.

Gutsche, J. (2009)

Genuine or Not ?

I'll show you a genuine smile!

Should I stick out my tongue?

I love pictures!

Smiles everyone!

I can't...hold it ...any longer....
Take the picture!

www.fourward.ca

FRESH SolUtions 2 Re-Cre8 Play

CREATE YOUR PLAY LAB

Look at your home or office as a lab, the mad scientist that you are, a scientific experiment awaits. Slip into something more comfortable, a white lab coat perhaps, make observations, take notes, experience and reflect.

Create a hypothesis and gather the data. Test out play theory. See if you get the same results as the American Academy of Pediatrics, with adults or teens.

Communication class: a mandatory course all students have to take at College and I had the privilege of teaching it. Thought if I could make it fun, engaging, we could learn a lot together. So we created a communications lab. Every day we met, tested theories, practiced, experienced and reflected...observation experiments, nuggets to practice (smile at everyone in the gym, lead a conversation with silence, stare at someone in the elevator...mirror behaviour) We learned, laughed and played a lot. It was one of the BEST CLASSES EVER!

www.Thefuntheory.com ✓ out their 2 min. videos: piano stairs, bottle bank arcade, world's deepest garbage bin. Creating stairs that looked and sounded like a piano when walked on, increased the use of stairs by 66% proving that fun and creativity changes behaviour!

Fail every day & Bite the moon (a French phrase meaning to **try the impossible** Bhalla, 2009)
"I've missed more than 9000 shots in my career. I've lost almost 300 games. 26 times I've been trusted to take the game winning shot and missed. I've failed over and over and over again in my life and that is why I succeed." Michael Jordan
In "Exploiting Chaos" the authors report that Microsoft waits until someone has one big public failure before promoting them!   **When was the last time you were promoted?**

SPLASH COLOUR
CREATE an EX PERIENCE!

Time to play
Schedule in a play date every week. Alone or with others, consciously go on an adventure every day. It could be as small as using a different coffee mug or painting your door purple. Maybe a little more extreme like lying down on the floor and looking up at the ceiling to day-dream at work.

Got one for ya, So Superman was flying to a superhero conference an

Oh no, your not going there!

Super Heroes

Superman never made any money, but he sure had fun flying. Batman had all those nifty gadgets and a Bat Mobile! Wonder Woman had the lasso of truth and the super powerful designer jewelry, not sure what those bracelets did. Who is your favourite Super Hero? And if you could be any of them who would you be and why?

Using the lens of a superhero to problem-solve can be interesting at a Board meeting. Donning a cape or mask leads to some pretty interesting dialogue and solutions!

Purse and Pocket

What you can do with a few every day items. There's a website where you can buy a facilitators kit that includes nothing but odds and sods like paper clips and wooden blocks, nuts and bolts and woolen socks, string and similar things. Items that you could pull together from your garage or workshop or purse or pocket. Use what you've got to perk up your play quotient. Do it now, dig in your purse or pocket, pull out three things. Use these items to nudge your creativity. You could be the next successful entrepreneur on The Dragon's Den!

Be proud of your play, of your creative nature, of your goofiness.

"It is utterly false and cruelly arbitrary to put all the play and learning into childhood, all the work into middle age, and all the regrets into old age."

Margaret Mead

Work & Play

To play or not to play, that is the question.
Whether thou shalt play at work or work at play matters not.

It is hereby decreed that once a day we must play.

corporate training

innovations involve

improv theatre techniques and game design technology

(http://www.soulview.com)

Play is primal, seek out play in nature, for by nature all shall see that play is the foundation for life.

www.fourward.ca

Top Reasons to Play at Work

from Linda Naiman www.creativityatwork.com

1. Play is the path to fun and profit.
Play opens up new channels of creativity and increases the level of satisfaction we experience at work. How employees feel about their company is directly related to their level of productivity and creativity. Research shows that highly motivated employees are up to 127% more productive than averagely motivated employees in high complexity jobs. — *Fortune Magazine*, January 1998.

2. "Fun is the new status symbol."
Studies show, if you want to attract and keep talent, you need to have a fun, challenging and creative workplace environment. It's your talent that sets your business apart from the competition.

3. We need time to be idle.
Taking time to do nothing lets problems incubate and allows for creativity to flow. Children who are allowed to daydream develop a higher IQ.

4. Play helps us find our genius.
Our childhood passions are the key to our genius. In the midst of play we experience unlimited possibilities.

5. Play is crucial to attaining a work/life balance.
A work/life balance (not money) is the number one concern of employees at all levels, in Canada and the U.S. The ability to achieve this is the top determinant in whether they are happy on the job, and whether they stay or leave.

6. Play is smart corporate strategy for solving problems.
Play frees us from worry and stress, relaxing the brain and making it easier to be more creative. Solutions that seemed so evasive earlier now appear effortlessly in the midst of play.

7. Play keeps our passions alive in the workplace.
Studies show, if you want to attract and keep talent, you need to have a fun, challenging and creative workplace environment. It's your talent that sets your business apart from the competition.
*Source: *Report on Business Magazine*, Aug. 1999

www.fourward.ca

1

8 years of your life
In 2008, approximately 10% of the total time available to all Canadians was devoted to paid work.

15 years of your life
Work 60 hours per week from age 21 to age 65 and you'll spend over 20% of your life working.

🕐

168 hours in a week
40 hours of work
56 hours of sleep (8 hours is ideal)
72 hours left for obligations (childcare, grocery shopping, cleaning house, religious commitments), personal care (eating, hygiene), driving, volunteering and of course Recreation and Leisure.

MINUS 35 hours of leisure (Canadian average with help from Stats Canada)

37 hours left for obligations, personal care and the others.

168 hours/week
60 hours of work
56 hours of sleep
52 hours left

MINUS 35 hours of leisure

22 hours left for everything else.

168 hour/week
80 hours of work
56 hours of sleep
32 hours left

MINUS 35 hours of leisure

(– 3) hours
No time for obligations.

What suffers?
Sleep, leisure, your health, well- being...

Just the Facts Mam

Ya numbers woohoo.. You know, recreation professionals have been warning of the ill effects of a lack of activity for over 20 years and it's just now that we are in an obesity epidemic that people are starting to listen

WARNING

Facts and numbers, now I can relate to that! Whoa, check out the warning, Is she serious?

All work and no play leads to a less satisfying life. You will suffer, your family will suffer, your kids will get into trouble, your house will fall apart, you will slowly waste away because you're not eating and sleeping. You will burn out, get depressed and feel unfulfilled. Give time to your leisure, play every day.

outcreate

outwork

THRIVER

Outplay

All work and no play makes Jack...is it a dull boy? Could it be a survivor?

Integrating play enhances

Working & playing with colleagues leads to Outcreating beyond your wildest imagination.

team building.

Talia Shafir, a regression therapist and co-founder of the Center for Integrated Therapy in Sebastopol says we're in survival mode and that we're doing good at surviving so it's time to move from survival **decreases stress** and to creativity. Money helps us survive, so how do we do this? Recognize we're in survival mode & make a conscious decision to move our perspective.

"Life needs creativity to thrive and the creative process needs acknowledged space to happen."

improves productivity.

How To Play at Work: The Buy-In

1. Start slowly, people may be leery or may want to integrate play but are unsure of how it will unfold. Warm up, walk before you run.

2. Transition people into and out of play with purpose. What's the purpose for playing?

3. People are familiar with brainstorming, it's a 'divergent' exercise and a great place to start. Use non-traditional brainstorming techniques (many available on the internet). This is the warm up, generating as many ideas as possible, quantity is king. Build new ways to approach situations.

4. Take the best idea that emerges out of play and develop it further (the 'convergent' mode). Seriousness kicks in because the realities of costs & resources, time & effort are weighed into the equation.

5. It's not either or, apply each at the appropriate time.

How To Play at Work: The Bat

Grab a bat – aluminum, wood, nerf, collector, whatever the design ask a guy in your next brainstorming session to hold it up when you're in generative mode. Problem-solving, generating alternatives, creative exploration, product design, for any of these situations use the bat as your prototype and ask people to play with the idea of the bat and how it could be used to solve, create, design solutions. Push the group to come up with 100 ideas in 10 minutes. Transition people into the convergent mode to develop the idea/product/experience out of what evolved from your 'batman' play.

How To Play at Work: The Bastard

There's always one in every crowd – Be the Bastard. Bring your playful spirit and create havoc. Bring the hottest stuffed peppers for people to eat, crunchy nuts and chew with your mouth open, top it all off with the highest fat, smooth ice cream you can find and maybe a little wine for after 4, well it's after 4 somewhere. Play loud music, wear perfume or spray the room with peppermint, or silly string, paint pictures on your wall or hang a monkey portrait in the entrance. Create the Best Bastard award because someone has to shake things up.

www.fourward.ca

How To Play at Work: The Space

Create an atmosphere conducive to play **to encourage play** – blocks and chalk with boards and walk ways with space   white or black or a graffiti wall. Does your   space change or stay the same? Move it around, put the boss at the welcome desk for a day, the administrative assistant in the corner office with windows, encourage and create a space that changes and inspires. Hold an impromptu painting party during work hours. Include paint and pop and   space   to create. Big tables, tools, powered and cool. Creative and cool attracts creative and cool.

How To Play at Work: The Slide

Install a PING PONG TABLE, SLIDE, LADDER, BUNK BEDS, GOURMET KITCHEN, ROPES COURSE. Many of the leading creative companies have, did or are. Great for adding active distraction, brain breaks and colleague coolness, slides and bunk beds transform how our brains think about work and how we feel about going to work. As Canadians grow older they report the reason for going to work is not for the money but because they enjoy what they do. Bricker & Wright of Ipsos Reid in "We know what you're thinking" 2009. To engage the creative sector slides and ping pong tables will be standard equipment to build that sense earlier in a person's career.

The Place: Space & Slide Combined

Television:

Oprah, Jay, Ellen and David, Jon you too, why are your audiences sitting in front of you?

Theatre:

Charlton, Liza, Charlie (Chaplin), Shakespeare
"Theater structure is a critical part of a play." It encourages the way the audience experiences the play. Shakespeare had the 'Pit' with a fierce crowd fueled by plenty of wine. This is where the Elizabethan Commoners, referred to as groundlings, would pay 1 penny to stand. The gentry would sit in the galleries using cushions for comfort. Rich nobles could watch the play from a chair set on the side of the stage itself.

Early theatre structure consisted of two or more doors opening onto the apron where actors made their entrances and exits. Some of the audience would sit very near actors having to interact with them while coming on and off the stage.
http://www.william-shakespeare.info/william-shakespeare-globe-theatre.htm

www.fourward.ca

Playground Seating

Imagine walking into a theatre to watch Cirque du Soleil, a Shakespearean play or the Ellen Degenerous show. Instead of finding rows of chairs you walk into a child-like playground with monkey bars, giant swings, quad teeter totters, balance beams, playground equipment to hang on, swing from, balance on and interact with. How would that change the experience? Create a unique audience experience by creating a playground. Movie theatres are fast being replaced by pay per view, video rentals and stay at home options. Bring crowds out to take part in an experience.

Movies: Lie down theatre in Brisbane, Australia

Susan (Sarandon), Goldie, Samuel, John Cleese, George, and Brad. Clint, Jody, your movies are moving and entertaining it is so sad, that audiences are staying home to watch. How about creating a home away from home experience with catering to boost business. In Brisbane Australia they're doing just that. You walk into the theatre, order drinks (alcoholic and non) and food beyond the popcorn and Twizzlers, warm wings and burgers, hors'dourves of all kinds. You also choose what you'd like served as the movie starts and delivery half way through the show. You walk into the theatre and choose the pair of lazy boys where you and your partner will enjoy the show. Prior to the movie the wait staff bring your order, as you sink down into your recliner the movie starts. Half way through they replenish your drinks and food. Fabulously creative, what an experience! Taiwan has in-house video viewing...

At the

Go gle
office in York,

they supply all sorts of goodies to keep the creative juices flowing.

Retain creative workers!

Office space

Designers of Electric Works office complex in Sheffield, England, have come up with a novel way of lifting morale **d**uring the economic **d**ownturn. They have installed a see-through helter-skelter to take staff from the third to the ground floor reception area in an exhilarating **seven seconds**. Catering for media-related businesses, the novel **d**escent is made of steel and plastic, is 87ft long with a 40ft **d**rop. **D**esigner Toby Hyam, says it is intended as a 'statement about **risk-taking**'.

"I am not a Starfleet commander, or T.J. Hooker. I don't live on Starship NCC-170... [some audience members say 'one'], or own a phaser. And I don't know anybody named Bones, Sulu, or Spock. And no, I've never had green alien sex, though I'm sure it would be quite an evening. [Pomp and Circumstance begins playing] I speak English and French, not Klingon! I drink Labatt's, not Romulan ale! And when someone says to me 'Live long and prosper', I seriously mean it when I say, 'Get a life'. My doctor's name is not McCoy, it's Ginsberg. And tribbles were puppets, not real animals. PUPPETS! And when I speak, I never, ever talk like every. Word. Is. Its. Own. Sentence. I live in California, but I was raised in Montreal. And yes, I've gone where no man has gone before, but I was in Mexico and her father gave me permission! My name is William Shatner, and I am Canadian!"

William Shatner

LEAD

survival to creativity

From wherever you are
make a conscious decision to move from

Shape life creatively.

The pipe cleaner represents YOU. do.

Take a **pipe cleaner.**
Don't wait

Shape it.

for others to tell you what to

Shape it yourself.

It's that easy

"If you want creative workers,
give them enough time to play."
John Cleese

RISK

**danger, jeopardy, peril,
hazard, menace, threat,
possibility**

we are all leaders

take the risk first **as a leader**

Create your own creative play ideas, steal mine, steal others. Modify and make your own.

93

Here come the Fuzz

How to Create Purposeful Play at Work

Get Fierce and Have Fun

During court sessions it is common practice to take a RECESS. When in elementary school it is common to have RECESS in both the morning and afternoon. **Why is it that RECESS is relegated to judges, lawyers, criminals and children?**

Take a RECESS, coffee breaks are for common suits.

Play with words: common vocabulary is filled with four letter words and grade 4 comprehension. Expand lungs with language that creates fresh perspectives. Team leader replaced manager, customer engagement replaced customer service, we change words to reflect different types of leadership and interaction. Team leader might now be replaced with équipe Maestro (team genius). Teacher might become 'Analysis Facilitator' as we move beyond the information age into the age of critical analysis. Use metaphors; doing a puzzle is like teamwork, both need someone to move the pieces, having the big picture helps, each piece plays a specific role in the situation, the whole is more than the sum of its parts.

www.fourward.ca

Use structured unstructured play: Try Pauze Play – take 5 seconds before answering anything. **Try News Views –** read the first page of the newspaper or news highlights on a website, over the course of your morning use headlines in all interactions. **Try Eye Lights** –study your colleagues' and clients' eyes as if you were an Iridologist, discover the depth of colour in the iris, the dots and lines. Iridology claims that iris patterns, colours and characteristics reveal information on systemic health (no scientific evidence to these claims), the eyes certainly reveal 'tells' or 'Visual Accessing Cues' shown in Neuro Linguistic Programming (NLP) experiments.

Puzzles: Pick up a blank puzzle at the art store, work with your team to fit project design, systems or results together on puzzle pieces. Frame it. Bring an oversized puzzle of the world with BIG pieces to the next business briefing, use it as a visual and kinesthetic exercise in updating the growth of business globally or expansion plans.

Tom Kelly of Ideo has built many profound sentences around interesting notions. One notion I particularly like is the one that nudges others to

PLAY WITH CONSTRUCTION – Thinking with hands

Tom hit the nail on the head, he said that building and thinking stuff is **taken away from us** as we get older, so when we're in kindergarten we've got easy access to all sorts of construction materials and tools, paints and cardboard, building blocks and toys, kites and string and probably even a turtle pond. Their ability to prototype is instant.

How much stuff
- do you have within reach of your desk?
- do you see that you you could use to prototype with?
- is within a 10 second jog of where you usually work?

What can you do with 11-4" Nails and a block of wood?

Pound 1 nail into wood so that it sticks up 3 ½"

Now try to balance the remaining 10 nails on top of that nail without any of them touching the wood. It is possible.

Answer 1 page away.

Check out the Serious Play video on www.TED.com He uses finger blasters to develop creative solutions

Building Blocks – put them on your desk
One study found kids who played with blocks **scored higher on language tests** than kids who didn't. Maybe the children with blocks spent less time on unproductive activities still blocks were good for them.

Lloyd Smith Solutions uses LEGO® Serious Play™ to build business solutions. From team building, problem solving, strategic planning & change management, to succession planning, innovation mining, branding, communication, high scope analysis & action planning they're serious about play.

Cardel Place

gives the gift of play

An exemplary example!

"Our role is to:

Provide an experience for the mind and body to play."

Where's Cardel Place?

Calgary, Alberta, Canada, need a map? It's sandwiched between British Columbia and Saskatchewan U know the wheat fields and the 2010 Olympics?

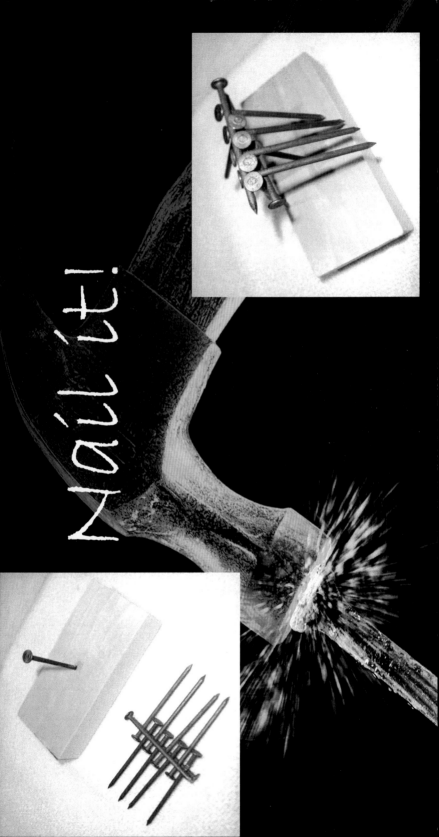

Nail it!

SHOW TIME – DRAMA 101 – The Service Industry

Drama Please! Comedy, Thriller, Action, Mystery, whatever the service that's provided (education, sport/wellness, healthcare) it's all about the **experience**. Start acting, making movies and designing sets 'cause the entertainment industry is moving in.

To meet the needs of clients, customers service providers need to act out the scenario to find what works.

If Frankly my dear, you don't give a damn, service quality will feel it.

Enroll in Drama 101: training + experiencing the service from a customer perspective = understanding the client situation ~ Standing Ovation, **Bravo!!!!**

Try **Invisible Theatre** – where you play the customer in a REAL WORLD SITUATION but no one else knows you're acting. For example: Sit in a waiting room for 6 hours with others hacking and moaning beside you if you're a hospital administrator. A town planner? Donne a wheelchair during the winter and see what you have to contend with on downtown streets. Make a movie to remember that adventure, analyse it and do wheelies when you figure out solutions.

Educators use role play, labs, clinics and other **experiential methods** to immerse students into the REAL WORLD. Estheticians and massage students practice on each other, on friends and family. Nursing students give needles to each other. Leadership classes create group scenarios to challenge leadership within groups. Organizations, businesses and workplaces in general can use the same methods to move the one RESPONSIBLE from the OFFICE Window closer to the customer. And YES it's play, **ROLE PLAY.**

Put on your tap shoes, you're going to Broadway. Drama 101 is basic training for the workplace. Roleplay identifies rules for social interactions which can be studied if captured with

Video, like taping your presentation and dissecting it afterward, video a clients experience from their perspective to "try it on."

www.fourward.ca

ACT CRAZY

DO wild and crazy things

Especially if you're a owner, a senior manager or team leader, it

Increases the likelihood of others taking risks and

builds trust (that's what Gutsche says in "Exploiting Chaos", LUV that book!)

INVEST in ACTING

103

Investment makes sense. Improv rules make sense 4 business

Ten Commandments for Improv Theatre (from improv encyclopedia group)

- Thou shalt not block
- Thou shalt always retain focus
- Thou shalt not shine above thy team-mates
- To gag is to commit a sin that will be paid for
- Thou shalt always be changed by what is said to you
- Thou shalt not waffle
- When in doubt, break the routine
- To wimp is to show thy true self
- (S)he what tries to be clever is not; while (s)he that is clever doesn't try
- When thy faith is low, thy spirit weak, thy good fortune strained, and thy team losing, be comforted and smile, because it just doesn't matter.

⚡ **Understand the rules**

⚡ **Master the rules**

Bre⚡ak
them

not just because, but because they are limiting movement, limiting learning, limiting your core principles, limiting something you are not willing to compromise.

105

Meetings

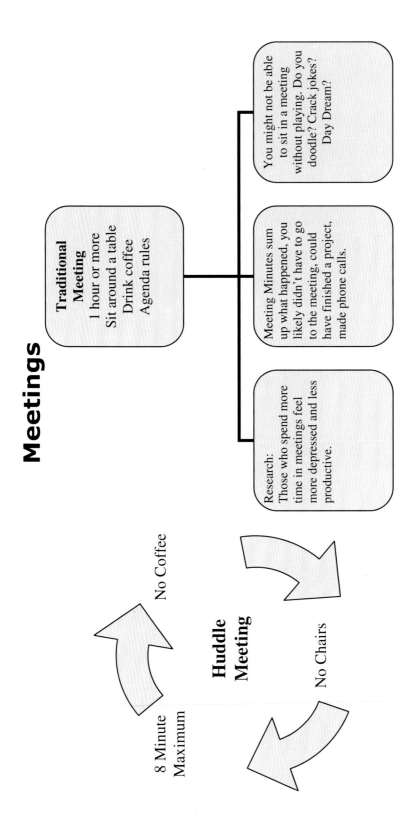

Traditional Meeting
1 hour or more
Sit around a table
Drink coffee
Agenda rules

Research:
Those who spend more time in meetings feel more depressed and less productive.

Meeting Minutes sum up what happened, you likely didn't have to go to the meeting, could have finished a project, made phone calls.

You might not be able to sit in a meeting without playing. Do you doodle? Crack jokes? Day Dream?

No Coffee

8 Minute Maximum

Huddle Meeting

No Chairs

For traditional meetings that you're not running:

Bring something concrete to do/play with.

Play word bingo http://www.keithandcompany.com/fg_lobby.html

Tools to help you stay awake in boring meetings:
http://www.ehow.com/how_5706314_stay-awake-during-boring-meetings.html

For meetings you run:

Take them running or walking outside.
Make your meeting short, 30 minutes max.
Get to the point, decide or take action and head out.
Hold a stand up meeting or a Huddle meeting http://www.keithandcompany.com/fg_lobby.html.
Buddy up, drink water and take washroom breaks often if you have lots to meet about.
Don't meet about anything you could send out in an email.

www.fourward.ca

Work to Recreate

or

Recreate to work?

Are you working so that you can take off skiing or so you can afford to travel?

Or are you using your leisure time to rejuvenate yourself so that you can go back to work?

Historically people worked to survive and that's still the case but where does recreation, play and leisure time fit in?

You might see your work as play – what more could you ask for!
You might see your play as work – professional athletes might agree.

Recreation, Play, Leisure Time is a RIGHT!

Consistent with the **Universal Declaration of Human Rights** (Article 27), all cultures and societies recognise ... the right to rest and leisure... personal freedom and choice are central elements of leisure, individuals can freely choose their activities, experiences.

All people have a basic human right to leisure activities that are in harmony with the norms and social values of their compatriots. All governments are obliged to recognise and protect this right of its citizens.
www.worldleisure.org

Right To Play
"Creating a healthier and safer world for children through the power of sport and play." Sport and play teaches important life skills such as teamwork, co-operation and fairness. Visit www.righttoplay.com
Play: Priceless

Josef Pieper says that **'Leisure is the whole point of life'** in his book *Leisure, The Basis of Culture.*

The British Columbia Therapeutic Recreation Association believes that recreation, leisure and play are inherent and significant aspects of the human experience as they promote quality of life and wellness at each stage of development.

Individuals of all abilities have the right to benefit from recreation and leisure.

(from their Code of Ethics)

http://www.bctra.org/node/9

☐ WORKOUT AT WORK ☐

Integrate movement into your workday by	Rather than	Comments; where to get equipment, what to do, general information
Walking on breaks or for meetings	Sitting in the coffee/boardroom	• Walking meetings enhance creative energy, help to break out of ruts and can MOVE a committee past obstacles
Walking while you work using a tread desk	Sitting at your desk for hours at a time	• Check them out at www.treaddesk.com • For a Canadian supplier www.instrideoffice.com • Advantages to standing up and walking while you work: - burn more calories/weight loss - increase heart rate - reduce back pain - relieves stress, anxiety, depression - walking is food for our brain - feel more alert and creative…
Taking the stairs to the coffee shop on the first floor or walking to colleagues offices	Using the elevator, phoning or emailing	• To communicate between floors or offices. • Face to face interaction is decreasing in work environments which impacts connections and effective relationships.

In your office have a mini medicine ball to play with (2–4 kg)		• Toss it to anyone who walks in your office. • Play idea 'it' when problem-solving. • www.fitter1.com
Put a balance board under your desk	Feet flat on the floor with no motion	• Rotate ankles and increase circulation. • Stand on it when you're eyes are square. • Standing on it works your proprioceptors. • www.fitter1.com
Sitting on a Swiss ball or a sit fit disc	Sitting in a chair	• In your office, board room or for conferences, provide them as an alternative to chairs. • Increases balance and use core muscles. • www.fitter1.com
Stand up desk	Sit down desk	• Elevate your workspace, keyboard, monitor. • This reduces the stress on your spine. • Sitting puts the most pressure on spines.
Skipping ropes long and short		• Enough space? Skipping invigorates. • Not much space? Skip sans rope as a group or alone. Or head outside. • Work on coordination by group skipping.

www.fourward.ca

Learning In the Classroom?

Who'd have thought

Exercise Balls

sharpen attention
improve posture

more than 300 schools are using exercise balls. Dr. John Ratey, a Harvard University professor says the tiny movements kids make while balancing **stimulate** their brains and help them **focus**. Children with attention disorders have "**a sleepy cortex**," and exercise combats mental disengagement. By using their core muscles they activate their brain. **Turning on** the prefrontal cortex inhibits impulses.

2009 experiment overwhelmingly indicated a preference for ball chairs

John Kilbourne, a Grand Valley State University (Michigan) professor of movement science, conducted the study with college students using exercise balls as chairs. They perceived an improvement in concentration and focus. Kilbourne is contacted every week by educators who want to use ball chairs.

Do You? I've got one in my living room, office & bathroom, okay not the bathroom yet.

Ellen Degeneres

Ellen comes dancing in to music of all genres. She & her audience groove for the first few minutes and at first glance it may seem strange, but you might just get up and start dancing yourself. It's a new era of talk show with Ellen's spirit of fun and movement. It's about playing. **Do You?**

Check out that table tennis paddle!

113

THE WINDOW WORLD

Do you have a **BIG** window in your office? The view is less important than what you do when you look outside and your state of mind.

It is the window to the world filled with **BIG** possibilities. It shows the ecological system with intricate linkages from earth and sky, vegetation and asphalt, access and transportation routes, work and home, business and consumer. It shows connections between people with places, consumers with products and people with people.

Out your window:
Stand up and purposefully look out to connect, think and feel.

Map out the connections that you see in front of you, how do people move, shift and interact? What would it look like if those patterns changed or if you were on the other side of the world? If you wiped out the view and began from merely the topography in front of you what would make the most sense? How does this relate to your work? Is it the organizational chart that is in need of re-thinking? Is it a new distribution system? Is it your marketing plan? Possibly internal operations? Whatever it may be translate what you see outside the window as a metaphor for your work situation.

Design this new system that you see emerging from what is outside the window with blocks. A 3 dimensional prototype is more realistic in systems design. We have **learned** to capture opinions & ideas in a two dimensional format with paper & pen. Now with computers we are able to three dimentionalize anything we desire. And that is a more realistic view of our world. So you can stay with old ideas and old technology, and old methods, however, to lead the pack, and you do want to lead the pack, or at least not get left behind,

you must be in 3 D!

If you don't have a window:

Create one for yourself or in every office so that everyone has a **BIG** window filled with **BIG** possibilities.

To create a window:
1. buy a picture of a window looking out or draw one.
2. take a picture of a window, blow it up & post it on your wall or **BLAST OUT THE WALL.**
3. have a friend paint a picture of a window on your wall
4. with staff design and develop how to put a window in everyone's office.
5. move to a workspace that has a window or no walls, offices looking inside and out.

www.fourward.ca

115

Mind

The Law of Attraction has gotten a lot of press since the film "The Secret", and the book by Australian television writer and producer Rhonda Byrne, took the nation by storm in 2006. After appearing on numerous talk shows, especially Oprah, anything on Oprah turns to gold, the notion that thoughts (conscious and unconscious) influence chance and can affect things outside of the head is believed true by many.

It's not a new notion, in 1879 the New York Times used the phrase to describe the wagon trains of the Colorado gold rush as "moving in obedience to some occult law of attraction that overcomes all obstacles in their progress to their destination". The *New Thought* movement beginning in 1904, used the phrase Law of Attraction to mean that if you really want something and truly believe that it's possible, you'll get it.

Of course there is skepticism from scientists claiming that it is impossible and violates scientific principles. And that's good because it pushes us to continue to dig deeper into this notion. Try it for yourself, if it works great, if not stop it.

Know that there's more to our being than what we know.

Because our minds are busy and we are a capable of thinking about several things at a time (some people can keep up to 7 lines of thought going in their minds, driving concentrating on the traffic, thinking about what to pick up at the store, what the kids are doing) it is difficult to focus solely on one thing, even when you try. Meditating is case in point. We have to practice, and practice repeating one sound or a mantra, over and over. Soon, unless you have practiced meditating for some time, your mind wanders. Our minds never stop working if you let them. Both take practice depending on what you've trained your brain to do. Some are in eternal zone out mode where not much seems to be going on at any time, but that's another state. Most of us have to concentrate very hard in order to stay focused for a long time.

Over

"Mantras are used as a technique for meditation. The idea is to keep the most active part of your consciousness busy, and at the same time let unconscious processes and lines of thought surface. This is similar to what happens in our dreams, but it has been proven that these meditation techniques can be more relaxing or cleansing than sleep."

If you're ready to adopt play to increase productivity here's how to start with a Mantra
Repeat for 5 minutes: Play produces, play produces, play produces.
It's like brainwashing yourself into believing, feeling, knowing and acting with purpose.

Mind

Team Trips, Travel and Social Trivia

Remember when you played volleyball or slo-pitch? Perhaps you were in band or a band. You traveled down the road together in a bus, ate together, slept together. There wasn't a moment that you weren't with, next to or near team mates. When you go on the road the group evolves. Structuring how it unfolds matters. Yes there will be tense moments and yes the group will need time to sort them out. Integrate play to invigorate, build team, productivity and creative energy.

Shared space vs your own space

If you're sharing space you get to hear snoring and bathroom antics, morning routines and evening secrets, **suffering succotash!** You must expose yourself a little bit more which may be uncomfortable. Plan fun food, pranks and adventures when your team travels together.

Your own space ... **MySpace** not THAT myspace

Keeps you safe and able to separate yourself, your work and home life, share what YOU want. Not necessary to expose yourself if you get to have your own hotel room rather than sharing one. Even still plan for ongoing encounters, evening events and breakfast bacon. Breaking bread breaks down barriers.

Events, Mini-tours, Retreats: Rock climbing, golf tourney, fundraising for a cause – Philanthropic activity dips new colours on old habits – paint houses for habitat for humanity or raise money for the United Way. People will pay to play if it's going to a good cause.

Pay for Scouting Vacations, a perk to pick up pebbles of wisdom. Trade employees, a trading tip to beat market retreats. Retreat to the ski slopes or campground for leadership bootcamp 101. Drills that will strip even the most seasoned leader of their ego. Ergo, Pick, trade and re – treat the group you work with.

Maybe they're coming. Ideas.

Is she doing this on purpose? So we realize patterns that have been normalized in society, to show that we are addicted to mediocrity? Or bored with it? Hmmm

Subscribe

To new ideas
To new magazines
To new newspapers
To new books, authors, thinkers, fields of study
To new music
To new television programs, movies
To new places
It's easy to get stuck in the doldrums. Make a conscious effort to get out

Surf

Surf sites you usually don't go to – use random key words. Edward de Bono, a creative thinking expert has a whole book dedicated to using random words to stimulate creative action, "How to Have Creative Ideas".

Random words

| Crokinole | aluminum | net | sandals | ham | cup | kennel |

Find a killer **magazine/newspaper shoppe** and scan. Go to a section that you never go to – I found "The World in Six Songs" by Daniel J. Levitin in the science section that I rarely visit. Go to foreign languages, Chinese newspapers. Buy 5 – 10, scatter them in the coffee room, on your desk, on colleagues chairs.

Visit the **library,** did you know in Calgary, Alberta, Canada you can buy a public library membership for $12 a year? For that you get access to all the books and magazines and movies and CD's that you can imagine, and online search engines that some of the best Universities use. You also can access library services, to help with business development, research, and a whole lot of knowledge based services.

Pop into a **used book store** like Bookmans (www.bookmans.com) all over Arizona, I happened on one in Tucson. For a fraction of the price you can stumble upon interesting old and new items. It also shows what people are giving up, have given up, notes and script, scraps of paper and business cards used as book marks from those who have read ahead of you. Return pieces of your collection to a used bookstore near you or create a lending library or an exchange library in your home or office.

The Daily Show with Jon Stewart and The Colbert Report that spun off are true brilliance in TV. These writers and comedians snatched late night glory from David Letterman and Jay Leno. Prior to the Daily Show there were late night television talk shows, sure there was choice, but the choice was of character not content. Canadians had already arrived at the comedic epicenter of bastioning political satire through The Royal Canadian Air Farce, This Hour Has 22 Minutes, and the Rick Mercer Report, but had not pushed into late night slots. The Daily Show's evolution of news reporting (I know, it's comedy but wouldn't you rather watch snippets of the politicians and other news shows reporting the 'real' news and laugh rather than dismally trail into desensitization of wars and death, financial destruction and corruption, global warming and environmental disaster, scandal and more scandal?) changed the face of late night viewing. Thank-you! I was getting bored!

I agree, there's a point, think of how it could be presented with Play in mind... a video clip here would be killer!

Stumble

Stumble upon something interesting. Spontaneity produces some of the most interesting experiences and adventures. I was visiting my sister in Tucson, Arizona and she suggested a trip to San Carlos, Mexico, a 6 hour drive away. Well the first night, New Years Eve we happened upon 'Froggy's a quaint little night club with live band. The only reason we got there was because we were in the right place at the right time. Running into some other Canadians, Albertans actually, they offered us a ride and we ended up playing pool, meeting trailer park people from our homeland, Manitoba, and other interesting Canucks, actors, developers and the such. One of them knew a friend of mine's best friend...6 degrees of separation.

We met the Fockers on our third night, an interesting crew of potty mouth partiers who were full of local tips. We were minding our own business at the beach club beside our residence, where the Bad News Blues Band from Tucson played, when the local cat introduced us. They were building a place in San Carlos, renting a home for $500 per month, and told us about deals of all kinds, the ones you want to make and the ones that you don't want to know about.

The fifth night, Silent Night, we thought a nice evening at the upscale establishment of 'Blackies' was in order, after cleaning up and donning our best attire, we headed out only to find that Blackies wasn't open Monday night. All dressed up and no place to go we headed off to find another place. We drove down to the marina, walked by the restaurant with white linen tablecloths we had seen earlier only to see one diner in the whole joint. It looked like she was a movie star who had rented the whole place so that she could dine in silence. I couldn't even approach the waiter for a table. It looked nice enough but more like a cafeteria in a large office building waiting for the lunch bell to ring so that all the white collar workers could stumble down, gulp down a couple of martinis and head back up to their corporate offices in the sky. Not far away was the Captains Club, Club Capitano. Our Silent Night continued but in a very different way. As we ate our pescado, one of the owners announced that silent movies would be starting outside in half an hour. We watched Charlie Chaplin and Buster Keaton as Fatty Arbuckle movies while an amazing piano player moved us through each scene. Only in Mexico!

Another Mexican experience in Buccerias: we went to a vegetarian restaurant. After our meal we sat outside on recliners and couches set behind the dining area, drank margaritas and watched "The Queen" on a white linen screen (bed sheet actually) that was strung between two palm trees.

I wonder when I'll be so lucky again.

I wonder when I'll be lucky to not have to read so much!

This creative connection stuff doesn't aim to throw out EVERYTHING that we've got. People need variety, the linear AND the lateral. This was a story, stories are Okay.

Steal

Tom Kelly in his book "The Art of Innovation" suggests **'idea wading'** as a way to promote cool, new ideas. He encourages people to go other places and 'steal' their ideas. As you may have noticed I've referenced many resources along the way. Each time I see links I build on them because the connections are uncanny. I saw an educational institution who used trips to art galleries and museums to link art and design with project management. It was truly innovative to see how they structured the design of study in order to expand the scope of student's experience and connect fields of study.

Stealing – **does it really matter whose idea it is?**

In this day and age there is a problem in traditional education with plagiarism because students do not seem to think that it is necessary to reference the information that they use. Information is so readily available that it's not necessarily as important as what's done with it and how it is transformed along the way to be useful in the context of the present situation.

"Borrowing Brilliance and Other Oxymorons" by David Kord Murray talks about the link between plagiarism and creativity. In the book, he explains "that there's a fine line between plagiarism and creativity—that creative thought begins with copying, that you build new ideas out of existing ideas, and that originality is a perception and not a reality. For me, this was a liberating insight that changed my relationship with creative thought. It prompted a renewed search for existing ideas and the illuminated the process of re-combining and re-structuring them to come up with a new one. And so, as I go out into the world and teach people about creative thought, I'm often asked by managers "how to" apply this in an organization. They want me to talk about "corporate creativity" and "innovation management" and at first blush, to me, "corporate creativity" seems like a Carlinesque oxymoron. It seems like two words that contradict each other, like "jumbo shrimp," "military intelligence" and "borrowing brilliance." Corporations are typically highly structured and highly political, and typically NOT very creative. But they don't have to be this way. In fact,

once you understand the basic mechanics of creative thinking, the basic block and tackling skills of the thinker, you can turn your organization into a creative factory that churns out innovative concepts through intelligent collaboration and the development of a corporate culture that fosters "corporate creativity."

It's less about what's mine is mine and more about community. Case in point: from individual computer use, information generation to Social networking sites and Web 2.0. How will this affect us in the future? And what do we have to do about it now so that we can see the opportunities that it affords us? Does it mean that we have to change our business models? You bet, look at how the music industry is scrambling to adapt and alter business models, lots of options on the go now.

"The secret to creativity is knowing how to hide your sources." Albert Einstein

125

www.fourward.ca

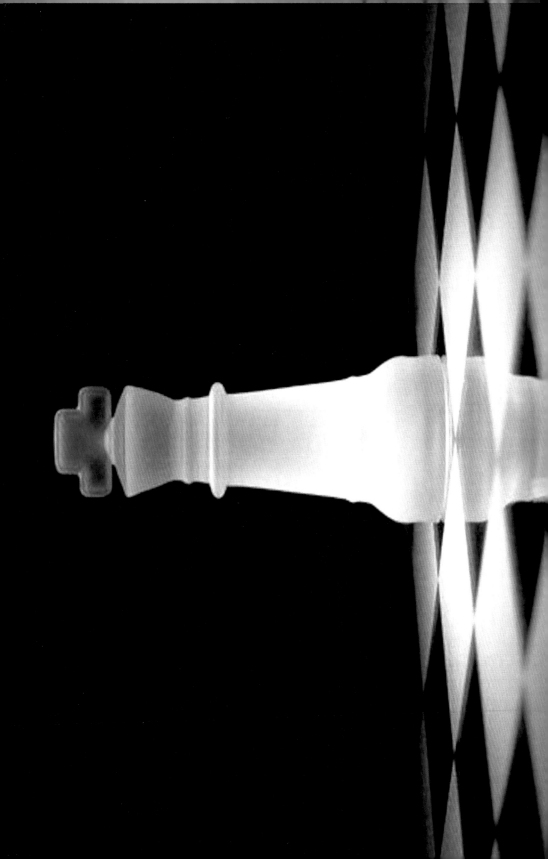

I failed
to make the
chess team
because of
my height.

Woody Allen

127

GENIUS TIME

I **stole** this one I think I first heard it from an executive coach. He said that I should work out a way that I could spend more time on my Genius time. When you're doing what you're **best** at, what you ❤, what rocks your 🏺, kinda like Csikszentmihalyi and Flow. Your **SEARCH** for the HOLY GRAIL 🌍 But Don Quixote found out that sipping water by the riverbank with a peasant **WAS** the HOLY GRAIL. *It's inside of you, in front of you, it is a part of you, here and now.*

Spend at least 20% of your work time on genius time, at least. **Google's 20% time for special projects** is not only encouraged, it's actively encouraged. Getting good 20% projects seem to be linked to performance reviews, they mean business, they want creative genius and won't settle for less.

Make it a policy - **The Genius Policy ~ *foUrward*** *I'm working on it, I'm working on it...* Be it proclaimed that all *fourward* initiatives are based on individual, collective or collaborative genius. Consider creative connections, passion projects, Flow Joe, that enhance and satisfy the genius and/or genius community, as the *fourward* core. ✹

Be Tall Enough!

If you think **play will never work** at work what chapter are you on?

Life in 5 Short Chapters *By Portia Nelson*

CHAPTER 1

I walk down the street. There's a deep hole in the sidewalk. And I fall in. I am lost. I am helpless. It isn't my fault. It takes forever to find a way out.

CHAPTER 2

I walk down the same street. There is a deep hole in the sidewalk. I pretend I don't see it. I fall in again. I can't believe I am in the same place. But it isn't my fault. It takes a long time to get out.

CHAPTER 3

I walk down the same street and there is a deep hole in the sidewalk. I see it there, and still I fall in. It's a habit. But my eyes are open and I know where I am. It is my fault and I get out immediately.

CHAPTER 4

I walk down the same street. There is a deep hole in the sidewalk. I walk around it.

CHAPTER 5

I walk down a different street.

Pull out the Board games kids it's time for a games night!

Use games at the office to problem solve, develop ideas, create space, build camaraderie and healthy competition. Bring games like Boggle, Taboo, Urban Myth, cards, dice, Conversation Starters, Wii. A few games I ran into that looked interesting are, **"What"** (it has WHAT questions that you ask others like, What people do when no one is looking, What is the best thing about a blizzard at Christmas (your in-laws cancel coming to dinner, you can snuggle in by the fire with loved ones) and another called **"Things"** Things your parents didn't tell you, Things you'd like to do.

Two that I played recently
- "Settlers of Catan" which is never the same game twice because the board you play on changes each time you play and changes with the number of players.
- "Citadels", you are a medieval ruler trying to complete your city before your opponents can build theirs. Expand your city by adding new districts.

These are both a little more sophisticated than the word games, good for strategy building. Check out your local games store.

Ball games like Dodge ball has come back in full force, for adults. Yep there are co-ed adult dodge ball leagues at University and in communities. Pure fun!

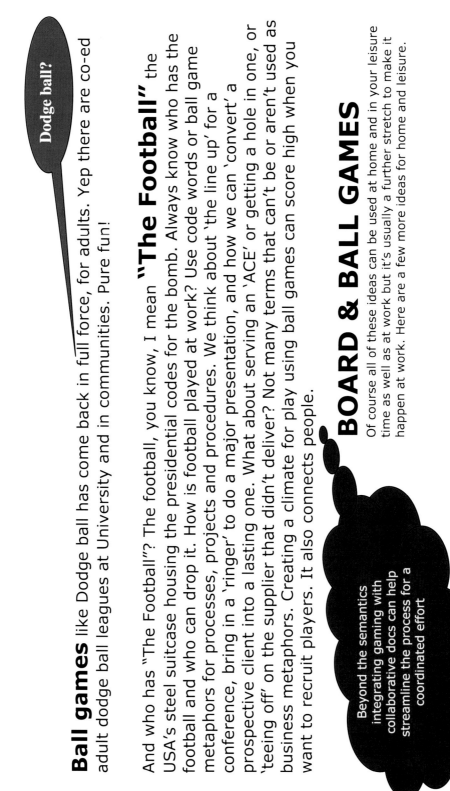

Dodge ball?

And who has "The Football"? The football, you know, I mean **"The Football"** the USA's steel suitcase housing the presidential codes for the bomb. Always know who has the football and who can drop it. How is football played at work? Use code words or ball game metaphors for processes, projects and procedures. We think about 'the line up' for a conference, bring in a 'ringer' to do a major presentation, and how we can 'convert' a prospective client into a lasting one. What about serving an 'ACE' or getting a hole in one, or 'teeing off' on the supplier that didn't deliver? Not many terms that can't be or aren't used as business metaphors. Creating a climate for play using ball games can score high when you want to recruit players. It also connects people.

Beyond the semantics integrating gaming with collaborative docs can help streamline the process for a coordinated effort

BOARD & BALL GAMES

Of course all of these ideas can be used at home and in your leisure time as well as at work but it's usually a further stretch to make it happen at work. Here are a few more ideas for home and leisure.

131

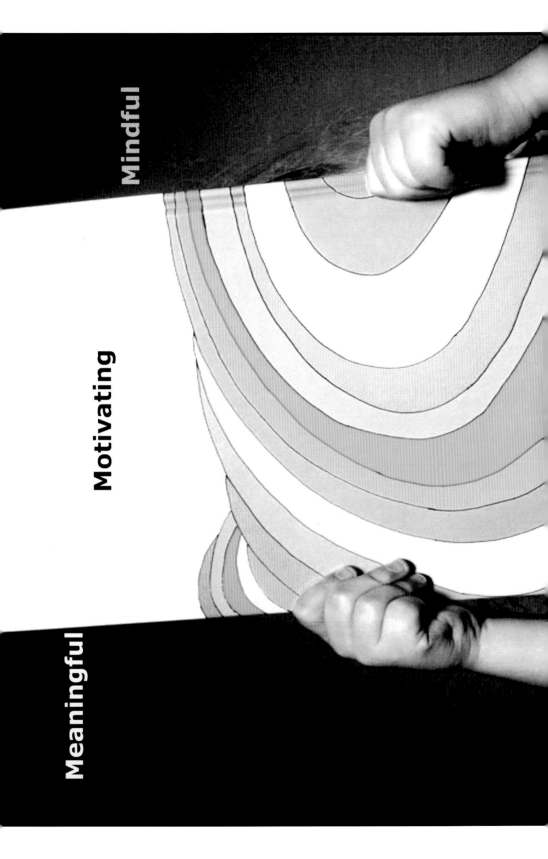

BOOKS

KIDS

I walked into "Suitcase" a web design company in calgary (www.suitcaseinteractive.com) and on the front coffee table sat "Oh the places you'll go" by Dr. Seuss. Unlikely books for unlikely purposes, if you don't have children or they've grown up look through the children's section at the bookstore, you never know what you'll find: brilliant colours, pop-up castles, new creatures and talking sponges. Great for gifts, children's books have hard hitting messages about societal issues, human interest and leadership, for the coffee table, or bed time reading. Some of the most popular authors are teachers, child psychologists and physicians. It's a very creative world that captures and inspires young minds, a perfect place to inspire minds that have been around awhile.

133

www.fourward.ca

Play at HOME

when you're supposed to be doing other important stuff like cooking, cleaning, fulfilling obligations that our family, friends and society

EXPECT

us to take care of like returning voice messages or mowing the lawn or grocery shopping. That's not to say that we shouldn't do all these things....

why not put them off, integrate play or at least approach them with a playful spirit.

In comes

Snow White and the 7 Dwarfs "Whistle while you work"

Sure sounds a little Pollyanna. Instead try a Marathon Whistle. With friends or family see how long you can hold a whistle without a break. If everyone starts at the same time it's highly likely you won't make it very far, like Underwater Hockey if everyone submerges at the same time you'll all come up for air at the same time, time your starts.

Can you name the 7 Dwarfs?

Play's Part for the Planet

a box and imagination can work wonders! Borrow, go to used gaming stores, online trading centres like Craigslist or eBay where you can find almost anything. **Don't just re-gift, re-think gifts, consumerism has us buying stuff all over the place, why?** Susan doesn't buy new stuff, only refurbished, recycled STUFF, **could U?**

Engineers ROCK! Change the use of what you've got, play with ideas to reuse items for DIFFERENT USES, a rug for a table cloth or art on the wall, red plastic table cloths for a red carpet (Thanks Rosie), tie downs for a computer holder, a stack of books for your night stand... Share it, give it away, turn it into something before you pass it to the recycle bin. **Barter** – Joan raises chickens in Tucson, trades eggs for other goods. What can you do in your backyard?

Home Movies and Mexican movie nights

Pull out your home movies and make a batch of popcorn it's **Movie Night!** Rent or borrow a few movies and invite friends over for a movie night, outside. Mexican influences for outdoor movie nights persist. String a sheet between trees or on an outside wall, set up the projector and host your own 'drive in'. Pull your old couch outside, comfy chairs, popcorn and Twizzlers of course.

135

www.fourward.ca

Goldie Locks chose the most comfortable bed for a snooze. Maybe she had Clinophobia (the fear of beds)

Charge the furniture manufacturers, if couches weren't so comfortable

we wouldn't have an Obesity Epidemic!!

Sit on the floor

What if couches were uncomfortable? It would be tough to be a couch potato because you wouldn't sink into that comfy couch...sitting on the floor is more conducive to who we are, standing is still the best for health. The average adult sits for over 90% of their day. **9 0 per cent !!!**

Track how many hours you spend sitting in a day.

Albertans compared to other Canadians are more likely to leave their laundry until they have no underwear left. That's a good thing, saving the planet's water and more time to play.

www.fourward.ca

Oh the Places You'll Go when you travel
to a place you've never been
Pick up a map
Local map
Bike map
Provincial map
World atlas

To gain more playtime
Say NO for 2 days
- with family (kids)
- for friends (goalie
- play as work (commissioned sculpture, training for Olympics)

To have a little more fun
Say YES for 2 days
- take an adventure a day
- mental sex every day
(DeBono says creativity is mental sex,
paint, sing, go to the museum, try something new)

"TV is chewing gum for the eyes."

Frank Lloyd Wright

TV may taste good at the start, but soon your jaw gets soar, the taste gets bland.

If you must watch TV MOVE IT! Create a playground in your home. Move your couch against the wall, bring out kids toys, blocks, your workout equipment...play equipment...move while you watch. Move your TV to the basement, have a room for games and fun with no TV.

How many channels do you have? How many do you need?

GET OUTSIDE

"Unlike television, nature does not steal time, it amplifies it"

Richard Louv – Last Children in the Woods Children in Nature

Create your own channels; climb mountains, take a sculpting class, test-drive sports cars, listen to live music. Best way I've found is to sit in a boat, the channel changes on its own.

Party on the side of the road

When you're driving cross country and need a break pull over to the side of the road, turn the tunes up and dance on the side of the road. A sister event to the renowned Chinese Fire drill of the '80's.

Party with your fish, dance in the kitchen, 33% of us are doing it anyway.

Host a
ROAD BLOCK
Party

Pick a sunny spot, block your street off and invite passers by over for a complimentary beverage.
You never know what it will lead to. Spontaneous fun sparks creative encounters!

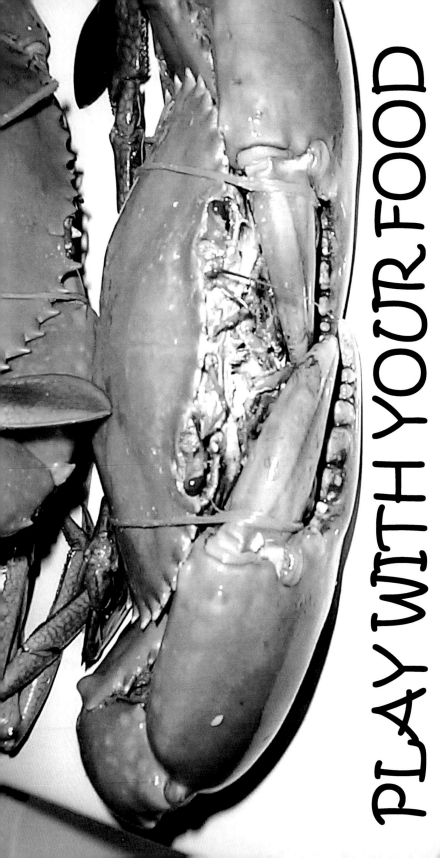

PLAY WITH YOUR FOOD

Sure Mom said Don't play with your food but here's the deal

The experience:

Create cakes of spectacular spectacle – the cake bake off with 5 foot high hat designs or my sister's rice crispy train cakes for her kids birthday, how amazing is that?

On your plate, toast turn into works of art with PB and Jam.

Shopping for the meal of the century is an event especially if a theme pulls it together.

The Anticipation of a meal makes our mouths water and when

The big event, meal, arrives tastes play with our taste buds if we try new flavours.

Once it's complete we remember and reminisce, laugh and sigh with satisfaction.

Heard of the SLOW FOOD MOVEMENT? Local foods, preparation, enjoying the experience of food and nourishment all at a pace that our digestive system was meant rev at. Not the fast food follies.

Hot dogs and pie eating contests move over, here comes the Chubby Bunny Champion, the gumball chewing champ, there's always room for more. Taste tests of worms and bugs, how would we ever know if these things were stomach worthy without brave souls?

Keep playing while you shop, prepare, eat and remember your dining delight.

www.fourward.ca

143

Music to my ears

I was in Las Vegas and was urged by my husband to visit the washroom. He had just returned from a visit and felt it rather imperative that I take my turn. Little did I know his motive was not entirely pure.

I walked into the Lou went into a stall as usual and took my seat as any young lady does when entering a space that is rather an odd place to share with the public. As I sat I noticed the music.

And so it was, playing in the Bellagio Hotel's grand ladies room the song titled "Bathroom" music by the Blue Man Group...how fitting, funny and unforgettable!

I now play the Bathroom Song in my humble bathroom when host gatherings. Not always noticed or commented on, I always get a kick out of preparing the continuous loop of music for my guests.

My husband? He takes no mind of the comings and goings in our bathroom but always spins the tale once he's visited and enjoyed the Bathroom song.

"Life must be lived as play."

Plato

www.fourward.ca

AMAZING WHAT A GAME OF HOCKEY CAN DO

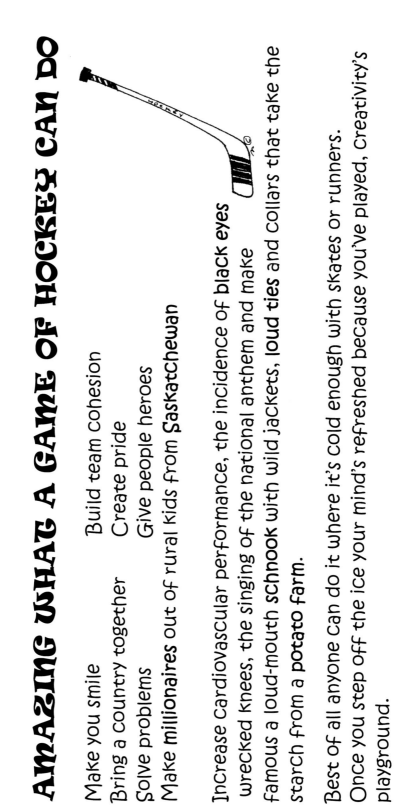

Make you smile | Build team cohesion
Bring a country together | Create pride
Solve problems | Give people heroes
Make millionaires out of rural kids from Saskatchewan

Increase cardiovascular performance, the incidence of black eyes wrecked knees, the singing of the national anthem and make famous a loud-mouth schnook with wild jackets, loud ties and collars that take the starch from a potato farm.

Best of all anyone can do it where it's cold enough with skates or runners. Once you step off the ice your mind's refreshed because you've played, creativity's playground.

www.fourward.ca

Model Creativity – Sure you can Use CLAY

Like in the movie Ghost with Demi Moore and Patrick Swayze that famous pottery scene, why was it so famous? You got your hands in wet muck, with stuff flying all over the place. Was it the freedom, the reckless abandon? My sculpting instructor Julie kept telling me to play with the clay when I was making a mask, change it, shape it, reshape it, keep changing it and it will evolve...Things don't always go how we think they will, it's about believing you can do it, trusting the process. We were sculpting a live model's head and he fell asleep after an hour, no one said anything, we all just kept going, smiling as his head bobbed but we didn't care, we were playing.

Make Paper Airplanes and take aim
"Do you aim low and hit or aim high and miss?"

Expect 100 blue items – I asked a group of students to count as many things they could that were red in the room, they had 1 minute. I asked who found 100, gasps, most people had between 10-20. Then I asked them to look for blue items, guess what, numbers hit the thousands (blue lines on paper) Brilliant!

Reasons to play: adventure, escape, belonging, physical health, mental health, risk, accomplishment, release, challenge, fun, COMPETITION, social connections, quality of life

Playing for the sake of playing is as fine a reason as any other.

Open the Door

Move over Dress-Up (Mr.) the Tickle Trunk's a changin'!

Mr. Dress Up, how old does she think we are?

Maybe she thinks we're wiser than our years, must be.

Tickle Trunk, toolbox, kit, stuff is fun, build a kit with:

Air, scented spray, food, smelly stuff ~ aroma therapy can spur focus (peppermint), relaxation (lavender), and energy (citrus scents)

Eyeglasses ~helps to see a situation through a different lens

My TOOLBOX changes all the time, sometimes it's stuff from around the garage, the kitchen, the drawer with all that junk in it or the bottom of my purse, the bottom of other peoples pockets and purses...No-I don't go digging in other people's purses, I get them to dig out 1 to 3 items that can be used as jumping off points for dialogue, brainstorming, creating links or prototypes.

It evolves based on the needs of the hour. A Play-kit can be planned or spontaneous.
What will your Tickle Trunk for play look, smell, feel like?

Done for now... look for **"Showgirl Trapped as a Librarian"** at <u>www.fourward.ca</u> go to **'About'** and click **'News'** to find the latest blog and more.

YES **U**

Florence Centre Plays 2 Connect Kids & Community

"The most touching story of this past year was integrative concert and Fashion Show in which children with **disabilities** being served by the Florence Centre were featured. Twenty years ago in Ukraine, parents were **ashamed** to have their children with disabilities in public. What a **change** this little program of the Florence Centre has made in the city of Zaporizhzhye. The **community** came together, **providing** free **transportation** for the families, **providing food** for those who attended after the **performance**, and **providing dance** groups to **perform** alone and **together** with these **special children**."

300 people attended

We support the Florence Centre

Parents and children felt special because it was done for them and with them.

Create Connections at <u>www.fourward.ca</u>